WARSHIPS ILLUSTRATED No 13

Cover illustration: *U-37*, under the command of Öhrn, enters her new home-port, Lorient, France, in August 1940. Although she has been repainted since her early patrols, the boat's original insignia, the legend 'Westward Ho!', is unaltered.

1. Returning to Salamis following her sinking of the battleship *Barham, U-331* flies an appropriately large victory pennant. On this same mission she had landed a commando team at Ras Gibeisa in Libya.

WARSHIPS ILLUSTRATED No 13

U-Boats of World War Two

Volume I

ROBERT C. STERN

a&ap
ARMS & ARMOUR PRESS
London New York Sydney

First published in Great Britain in 1988
by Arms & Armour Press Ltd.,
Artillery House, Artillery Row, London SW1P 1RT.

Distributed in the USA by Sterling Publishing Co.
Inc., 2 Park Avenue, New York, NY 10016.

Distributed in Australia by Capricorn Link
(Australia) Pty. Ltd., P.O. Box 665, Lane Cove,
New South Wales 2066.

British Library Cataloguing in Publication data:
Stern, Robert C. (Robert Cecil)
U-boats of World War Two.
Vol. 1
1. World War, 1939–1945 – Naval operations – Submarine 2. World War, 1939–1945 – Naval operations, German
I. Title.
940.54'51 D781

ISBN 0-85368-813-3

Edited and designed by Roger Chesneau.
Typeset by Typesetters (Birmingham) Ltd.
Printed and bound in Great Britain by The Bath Press.

◀2

2. The work for which U-boats were invented, the sinking of enemy merchant shipping. Here a large freighter is finished off by a torpedo from the single stern torpedo tube of a Type VII boat. Despite the popular image, most U-boat sinkings, at least in the first half of the war, resulted from surfaced rather than submerged attacks.

Introduction

The history of the war fought by the submarines (*Unterseeboote*, or U-boats) of the navy of Nazi Germany in the Second World War is a story of seemingly total paradox. Despite the great successes achieved by the German submarines in the First World War, the U-boat force of the resurgent *Kriegsmarine* was inadequately supported by the Navy's leadership. In response to the prewar predictions of the U-boat force, led by Karl Dönitz, that 300 submarines would be required to defeat Great Britain, the naval construction plans called for only 129 boats by 1946, and, as a result, Germany entered the war in 1939 with only 57 U-boats, of which just 26 were ocean-going types. Yet, with a force that was never large enough to permit the deployment of more than 20 boats at any one time until the middle of 1941, Dönitz was able to come perilously close to shutting down the Atlantic shipping lanes.

Equally parodoxical is the reputation achieved by the U-boats (and U-boatmen) in 1939–45. In popular propaganda the crews were bloodthirsty barbarians worthy of the Mongol hordes, stalking the sea lanes, murdering innocent seamen, shooting survivors, etc. To Winston Churchill and the British government they were the ultimate menace, not because they were cruel, but because they were very nearly successful. To themselves they were simply patriotic sailors, grimly following orders to fight the overwhelmingly strong enemy with the only tools available. The truth, as usual, lies somewhere in between. What is certain is that the successes achieved by the U-boat arm of the *Kriegsmarine* were gained at a terrible cost. Of 1,162 U-boats built by Germany before and during the Second World War, 632 were lost at sea, whilst of the 39,000 crewmen, more than 28,000 (some sources give figures as high as 32,000) were killed in action.

This volume covers the first half of the U-boat story, from the prewar rebirth of the submarine arm to the end of 1941. These were times of struggle and then of first success for Dönitz and his U-boats. It was the era of the great aces, of Prien, Schepke, Kretschmer, Schultze and many others. Above all, it was the period in which Dönitz proved his tactics, laying the groundwork for the even greater successes and devastating failures that were to follow.

This book could not have been produced without the help of a large number of U-boat veterans and naval enthusiasts who have assisted with photographs and information over the course of many years. These include Willi Brinkmann (*U-2* and *U-534*), Werner Hirschmann (*U-190*), John Albrecht, Gerhardt Beck, Wolfgang Hirschfeld (*U-109*), Ernst Schmidt, Wilhelm Spahr (*U-47* and *U-178*) and Eberhardt von Ketelhodt (*U-712*). Many others were equally helpful, including Ed Rumpf, Scott Van Ness and, especially, Ken McPherson. A number of institutions also must be mentioned as significant sources of the photographs that follow. These include the National Archives and Record Service (NARS) and the US Naval Historical Center in Washington, DC, and the US Navy's Submarine Force Library in Groton, Connecticut, whose staffs were unfailingly helpful.

Robert C. Stern

▲3 ▼4

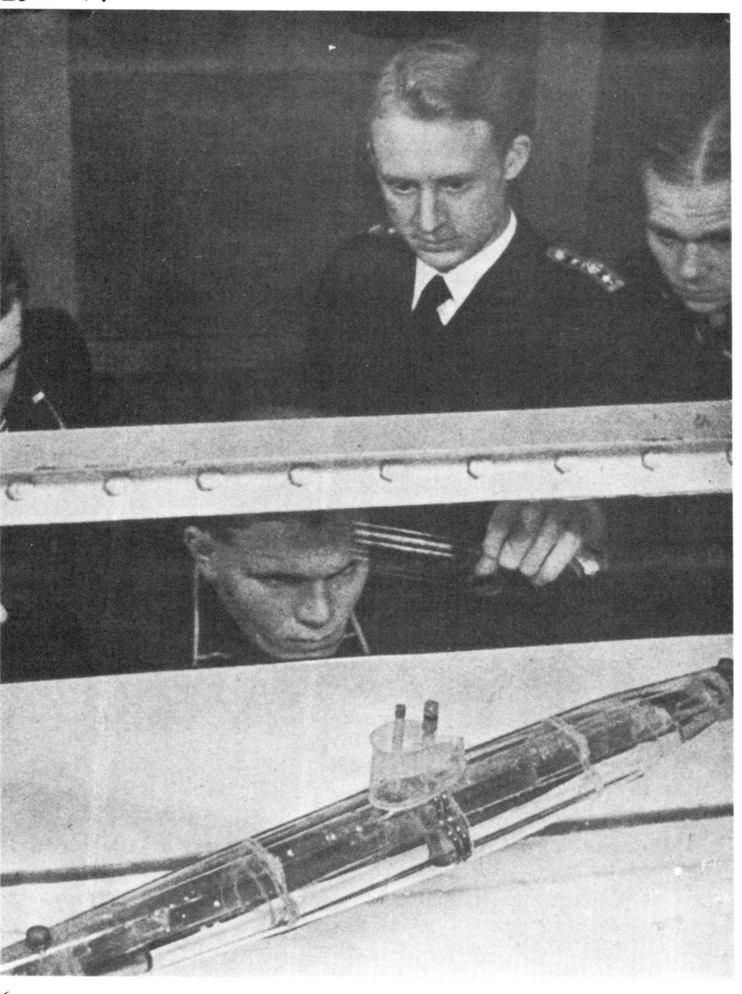

5▲

3. The Treaty of Versailles ending the First World War prohibited Germany from possessing submarines. However, even before the rise to power of the Nazis, German naval personnel were being secretly forwarded for training to commercial firms engaged in the design and construction of submarines in Holland, Spain and Finland. A number of submarine designs were produced and boats were built for Turkey and Finland. This photo shows *Vesihisi* in 1935, a Finnish submarine of the *Vetehinen* Class. This design was a follow-on to the highly successful UBIII design of the First World War and was to be the direct antecedent of the Type VII design. (Scott Van Ness)

4. While the first of the new boats for the resurrected *Kriegsmarine* were being secretly laid down in 1934, crews for the new boats were being trained at schools with sometimes deceptive names, such as the *U-bootsabwehrschule* (Anti-Submarine Warfare School) set up in 1933. At this institution the first crews were familiarized with the principles of submarine operation. At the beginning there were only models in tanks on which to train: the first real U-boats would come along late in 1935. (John Albrecht)

5. The first of over 1,100 submarines, the tiny *U-1* is seen soon after launch, late 1935. The early U-boat paint scheme consisted of light grey over ocean grey with the numeral in black. *U-1* was a Type IIA boat of just 254 tons displacement.

6. A Type II hauled out of the water on rails, showing the simple design of this class of coastal boat. Single-hull boats with midships saddle tanks for fuel and ballast, the Type IIs had three bow torpedo tubes and could carry six torpedoes over a maximum of 3,500 miles (for the late Type IID). These boats were so small that they were derisively nicknamed '*Einbäume*' (dug-out canoes). They were intended primarily as training boats for use only in the Baltic.

6▼

'. The number of available J-boats increased rapidly to the ›oint that it became necessary o establish the first U-boat lotilla (*1.Uflot 'Weddigen'*) in ›eptember 1935 under *Kapt*. Karl Dönitz. This view shows he first flotilla at its original ›ase at Pillau docked next to the irst of the submarine tenders, *'aar*. The second boat from the eft, *U-19*, is painted in the econd U-boat colour scheme, ›verall ocean grey with white ıumerals on the tower. (Via Ernst Schmidt)

. *1.Uflot* photographed some ime later. These earliest boats ıave all been officially edesignated school boats and ransferred to the submarine chool at Neustadt. Despite heir diminutive size, these Type II boats had all the same ypes of equipment as their arger successors and handled in nuch the same manner, making hem ideal training vessels. However, due to the extreme hortage of U-boats of any kind vhen the war broke out in 1939, nost of these early boats were ssigned to combat duty. (Via Ken McPherson)

'. A pair of young salts from *U-7* in prewar submarine utility lress of leather. Their cocky ppearance is not surprising: he new-born U-boat fleet ttracted only the most dventurous. The cap bands ndicate the boat's membership of *2.Uflot 'Saltzwedel'*, omposed of the early ocean-going boats.

◀7

8▲ 9▼

▲10

10. The earliest class of larger boats, the Type Is, was not particularly successful, and *U-26* was the second of only two to be built. The Type 1s were three times as large as the biggest of the Type IIs, and had twice the range, but suffered from very poor handling characteristics and were never repeated. (SFL)

11. The next design to be built, the Type VIIA, proved much more useful. While still deficient in range (VIIAs could sail only 4,300 miles), the boats were manoeuvrable and carried five torpedo tubes. They were small enough at 626 tons that many more could be produced than of a larger 'fleet' design, such as that favoured by the American and Japanese navies. By the end of the war, over 600 Type VIIs had been completed. Enlarging the external saddle tanks in later versions raised the range to 10,000 miles. (SLF)

12. One further design was built before war broke out, the ocean-going Type IXA. A successor to the large *U-Kreuzer* types of the First World War, the Type IX was larger (at 1,1032 tons) and had a better range (8,100 miles) than the Type VIIs, but it was less handy and dived more slowly. With six torpedo tubes (two aft) and 22 torpedoes (including eight stored in external deck-casing stowage tubes), they were powerful vessels. (SFL)

13. As war approached, exercises became increasingly realistic. A Type VIIA boat (possibly *U-33*) is seen here during Baltic exercises in July 1939. The simple prewar paint scheme has given way to an experimental camouflage of three tones of grey, and note the external aft torpedo tube characteristic of Type VIIAs; later marks carried this tube internally, allowing it to be reloaded. (Ken McPherson)

14. A U-boat at sea, silhouetted against a setting sun. This is another prewar view, as can be ascertained from the uncluttered 'as built' appearance of the tower structure and the fact that crewmen are scattered on the deck. At war, a U-boat would have only a limited number of personnel on deck and they would be concentrated near the tower hatch should it become necessary to crash-drive. (Via Ernst Schmidt)

▼11

12 ▲

13 ▲ 14 ▼

▲15

15. The outbreak of war in 1939 caught the *Kriegsmarine*'s U-boat force woefully unprepared for the ensuing struggle. Instead of the 300 submarines Dönitz believed would be required to wage a successful campaign against Britain, Germany had just 57, and that total included the unsuccessful Type Is and the short-ranged Type IIs. All the U-boats capable of reaching the British coast, a total of 43, were deployed as tension increased, most of them in a wide arc around the British Isles. Here a Type IIB leaves a German port on that first deployment. Except for the painting out of the hull number, she looks the same as she did prewar.

16, 17. The first 'success' of the war was a dubious distinction for *U-30* and considerable embarrassment for Germany. Despite explicit orders to follow prize rules strictly against merchant shipping, *U-30*, a Type VIIA commanded by Lemp, sank the liner *Athenia* without warning on 3 September 1939. Lemp did not report the sinking to Dönitz, and in the absence of information to the contrary German propaganda declared that the sinking was contrived by Churchill to inflame British passions. Lemp in his captain's white cap and officer's quality U-boat leathers (photograph 17), supervises the docking after that first patrol. Note the personal insignia, a jumping dog in white on a black circle.

▼16

17▲

18. Another early victor, much more to Dönitz's and the propagandist's liking, was Schuhart in *U-29*, another Type VIIA. On 17 September 1939 he caught the aircraft carrier *HMS Courageous* on convoy escort duty off the southern coast of England and sank her. While the sinking of high-value military targets was good for morale, and sinking aircraft carriers was always satisfying because aircraft were always the submarine's biggest problem, Dönitz knew that only by a concentrated attack on merchant shipping heading to or from England could the Battle of the Atlantic, so recently begun, be won.

19. *U-51*, a Type VIIB, traverses the Kaiser Wilhelm Kanal *en route* to the North Sea and war. She missed the earliest sorties of the war because she was undergoing a refit, the only visible evidence of which was the added spray deflector midway up the tower. She too sports a 'personal' insignia, black and white Scotty dogs in silhouette on opposite coloured circles and the slogan 'Atje Bambo'. Such insignia were applied at the captain's discretion, and most U-boats carried some similar form of decoration. (Via Ken McPherson)

18▼

19▼

▲20

20. Along with victories came losses. *U-40*, a Type IXA seen loading a torpedo, became one of the first combat casualties, striking a mine while operating in the English Channel on 13 October 1939. Three survivors were made prisoner. This was her second patrol; her first had taken her down to Gibraltar, where she attacked a convoy on 5 September. Note the patchy splinter camouflage of dark grey against the overall ocean grey. The insignia is a black umbrella.

21. One of the more famous boats, *U-37* (a Type IXA), prepares to dock after her first patrol commanded by Schuch, 15 September 1939. This patrol was abbreviated following a policy decision by Dönitz to deploy his limited resources in 'surges' (triggered by corresponding surges in shipping activity) rather than trying to maintain a constant number of boats (at most between six and eight) on patrol at all times. Nevertheless, despite the shortened patrol, Dönitz was disappointed that Schuch achieved no victories. (SFL)

22. For its next patrol, off Gibraltar, *U-37* was given to a new captain, Hartmann, and the results were dramatically different, with eight claimed victories for a total of 35,000 tons. Here victory pennants giving the name of each victim fly from the boat's periscope. The small pennant flying from the short mast to the left of the periscope carries a black cross, indicating that Hartmann was designated tactical commander of all Atlantic boats.

23. *U-35*, a Type VIIA, was another early war loss. She was depth-charged and sunk by a trio of RN destroyers east of the Shetland Islands on 29 November 1939 during her second patrol. Her successful first patrol had accounted for five ships totalling 16,000 tons. (SFL)

24. The autumn of 1939 faded into one of the coldest winters on record. German North Sea ports iced up for the first time in many years, making the U-boats' lives even more dangerous. Here *U-25*, one of the two Type Is, negotiates the still thin and patchy ice at Wilhelmshaven early in the winter of 1940. Note the more 'official' looking camouflage of connected dark grey patches on the ocean grey base.

▼21

22▲ 23▲ 24▼

25. Lemp's *U-30* returns from patrol on 17 January 1940. Icicles hang from the railings and overhangs, testimony to the frigidity of the weather. This had been primarily a minelaying mission off Liverpool, but *U-30* had sunk a Royal Navy patrol vessel and had claimed a hit on the battleship *Barham* – hence the miniature White Ensigns flying from the periscope.

26. At its worst, the ice made movement around Germany's North Sea ports nearly impossible, and here *U-37* is able to enter Wilhemshaven in February 1940 only because one of the *Kriegsmarine's* old pre-dreadnought battleships has acted as an icebreaker. The submarine is returning from a special mission during which she landed a pair of agents at Donegal Bay, Ireland, on 8 February.

▲25 ▼26

27▲

28▼

27. *U-25* returns from operations in the North Channel in February 1940, having sunk the Norwegian steamer *Songa* and five other ships totalling over 27,000 tons. Note the lifebuoy from *Songa* hanging from her tower, and also that a personal insignia, a red-capped mushroom, has been added since she was last seen (photograph 24). As commander of *U-25* and later *U-103*, Viktor Schütze (in the white cap) went on to become the third most successful U-boat commander of the war.

28. A tug helps *UA* make its way through the ice. *UA* was a large minelaying submarine which had been completing at the Germania Werft yard for Turkey (as *Batiray*) when war broke out. Taken over by the *Kriegsmarine*, she could be distinguished from the Type IXs which she resembled mechanically by the postioning of the deck gun in the tower structure and the cutaway deck casing forward (a feature repeated in the Type IXD2s in order to reduce diving time). (SFL)

◄29

30▲

29. The most successful boat of the war, in terms of tonnage sunk, was *U-48*, a Type VIIB: under three different captains she sank 53 ships totalling over 318,000 tons. She is seen here taking on provisions prior to setting off on a patrol during the depths of the winter of 1940, (note the ice completely covering the channel in the background). She carries a boat's insignia on her tower, a black cat with '3X' beneath, as well as a number of temporary markings related to the successes of previous patrols. On the port side of her tower she has her current claimed tonnage figure (115,000 tons) in large white numerals; on the starboard is a cartoon.

30. A close-up view of the cartoon on *U-48*'s tower shows a drawing of Schultze, the boat's captain, being chased by an angry Winston Churchill, leaving behind a mass of sinking ships. Such extravagant temporary artwork was not uncommon on *Kriegsmarine* vessels.

31. The object of all this attention was Herbert 'Vaddi' Schultze. He commanded *U-48* until April 1940 and then again for six months in 1941, ending up as the fifth most successful commander in that short time.

◄31

▲32

32. A number of U-boats, including *U-48*, experimented with temporary bow-caps to try to prevent ice damage during the hard 1940 winter. Here, with the weather warming, the bow-cap is being removed by workmen. All temporary markings seen in the previous photographs have disappeared, in their place a small white marking giving the tonnage sunk (115,000) just visible under the '3X' on the tower.

▼33

33. *U-25* loads a torpedo in preparation for 'Weserübung', the operations in support of the invasion of Norway, early spring 1940. Her appearance has changed again: the splinter camouflage has disappeared, replaced by a whitewash stripe on the front of the tower, and the mushroom insignia has been revised, with a second, smaller one added to the pattern.

34▲

34. Torpedoes were loaded into '*Einbaüme*' tail-first (as opposed to nose-first for all other types). In this photograph, a G7 21in torpedo is being loaded into *U-59*. The insignia on the tower is the iron hand of Götz von Berlichingen.

35. The G7 torpedo gave trouble from the beginning of the war, but the Norwegian campaign brought the problems to a head. As with most other naval powers, the Germans had developed a magnetic pistol for their torpedoes, which was supposed to trigger the torpedo's fuse in the presence of a strong magnetic field, such as that surrounding a ship. When it worked as designed, this fuse allowed the aiming of torpedoes without the need to make depth settings based on the estimated draught of the target, because it was designed to explode the torpedo under the keel. But, as was the case with the other navies, the *Kriegmarine*'s magnetic fuse proved unreliable, especially in Norwegian waters where large iron ore deposits were found, and, as again was the case with other navies, the Germans were forced to abandon the magnetic pistol, going back to the simpler and more reliable contact pistol. This photograph shows a torpedo being stowed in one of the external storage tubes of a Type IX.

35▼

▲36

▲37 ▼38

36, 37. In theory, the Type IX's external tubes allowed these long-range boats to carry additional torpedoes that could be brought inside the pressure hull when there was room. The loading would be made through the torpedo hatch, an angled hatchway that permitted the weapons to be lowered directly into the forward torpedo room with a temporary block and tackle arrangement rigged from the tower. The least enviable job was greasing the 'eel' as it was lowered through the torpedo hatch. All torpedoes on board a U-boat had to be serviced daily, even those stored in the tubes.
38, 39. The off-duty crew stands in review on the aft deck as *U-37* comes into port after a patrol, spring 1940. Eight pennants and a miniature Union Jack indicates a successful operation. Under Hartmann (until May 1940), and later under Öhrn and Claussen, *U-37* was to become the seventh most successful boat of the war. Hartmann's personal insignia was the 'Westward Ho!' inscribed under the mid-tower spray deflector. The faded traces of a splinter camouflage scheme can be seen on the hull.
40. Easily the most famous of the early commanders was Gunther Prien, who led his *U-47* into Scapa Flow to sink the battleship *Royal Oak* in October 1939. Prien was described as being the 'perfect' U-boat commander, not overly bright or imaginative but incredibly single-minded and daring in his pursuit of enemy shipping.

39▲ 40▼

▲41

41, 42. Prien's boat was a Type VIIB, which was easily the most famous design of the war and included Endrass' *U-46*, Kretschmer's *U-99* and Schepke's *U-100* as well as *U-47* and *U-48* among the boats built. These views show *U-47* after a patrol in the spring of 1940. The decoration on the tower includes a temporary marking celebrating the sinking of 66,587 tons of enemy shipping and the ship's insignia, the 'Bull of Scapa Flow'. This design, created by Endrass, who was Prien's IWO on the Scapa Flow mission, was later adopted by 7. *Uflot* as the flotilla insignia.

43. Spring 1940 was the time of the aces, the period during which the great early U-boat commanders could operate largely unfettered by the restrictions of 'wolf-pack' tactics, when individual skill and courage was more valuable than group discipline. Typical of these early aces was Endrass, who took over *U-46* on 24 April 1940. He commanded that boat until it was retired to training duties in September 1941, and then took over *U-567*. He was killed when the latter was sunk with all hands in December 1941.

▼42

43►

▲44 ▼45

44. *U-46* at about the time that Endrass took command. This photograph was probably taken during the relaxed time just prior to the U-boat's departure on patrol. A tug waits patiently outboard of the submarine, ready to push her out into the harbour; officers have assembled on the foredeck and on the dockside for the perfunctory departure ceremony.
45. Endrass and *U-46* return in battered condition from a successful patrol in late spring 1940. The damage to the tower was probably caused by a collision with a target that unexpectedly changed course – this was always a risk when a submerged U-boat was operating close to zig-zagging targets. Note the 'Bull of Scapa Flow' insignia, carried by *U-46* because it was a member of *7. Uflot* and because Endrass was the original designer of the famous insignia.
46. Schepke (in the white cap) commanded *U-100* from her commissioning until she was sunk by British destroyers on 17 March 1941. Schepke stood out among the early aces as the most flamboyant, and he had a reputation as a hard drinker and womanizer. Given that U-boatmen in general were known for their ability to 'let off steam' between patrols, Schepke must have been exceptionally talented to obtain such a reputation!
47. *U-99*, rather haphazardly concealed under sheets of canvas awning, prepares to leave on patrol, 1940. Her commander was Otto Kretschmer who, as captain of *U-23* until April 1940 and then of *U-99* until its loss on 17 March 1941, sank more tonnage than any other U-boat captain in the Second World War – 43 ships for over 263,000 tons. Kretschmer's personality could hardly have been more different from Schepke's: he was a sombre, unsmiling character and his boat was virtually undecorated, carrying only a horseshoe for good luck on either side of the tower. His and Schepke's boats were sunk on the same day while attacking the same convoy. Schepke was killed, but Kretschmer was taken prisoner along with most of his crew and served out the war in British POW camps.

46▲ 47▼

▲49

48. (Previous spread). The dangers of getting too close: *U-9* returns to port with a damaged bow, May 1940. Despite Dönitz's intention to retire the '*Einbäume*' to training duties, the low number of U-boats available for operations and the slow rate of new construction forced the continued use of these small vessels in patrols in the North Sea and the nearby coastal areas.

49. A closer view of *U-9*. Note the outline of a large 'Iron Cross' welded on the tower side: *U-9* had carried this marking since before the war, when it was designated '*Traditions-U-Boot*', commemorating the U-boatmen of 1914–18 (*U-9* was the number of the boat in which Otto Weddigen achieved his first victories in the First World War). Three pennants bearing the silhouettes of the victims fly from the periscope; the middle flag represents the French submarine *Doris*, sunk on 9 May during a minelaying operation off Holland.

50. *U-9's* commander was Lüth, who as captain of this boat and three others (*U-43*, *U-138* and *U-181*) during the course of the war, was to become the second leading commander in terms of tonnage sunk – 46 ships totalling 228,000 tons.

◄**50**

51▲

51. *HMS Seal*, a large minelaying submarine of the *Porpoise* Class, was damaged by a mine off the coast of Sweden on 4 May 1940. The next morning a German seaplane found the submarine wallowing in the light swell, slowly taking on water aft. The exhausted crew surrendered, believing *Seal* to be sinking. In fact, she stayed afloat, was towed into port and was subsequently repaired and commissioned into the *Kriegsmarine* as *UB* on 20 November 1940.

52. Living up to its reputation as probably the most decorated U-boat, *U-48* is seen here at Kiel in the summer of 1940. The decorations show the current total of tonnage and a cartoon depicting an angel of peace (complete with olive branch) hovering over the water. This view was taken after the first of two patrols when *U-48* was commanded by Rösing. Nine victory pennants fly from the periscope, and the tonnage total has been increased 42,000 tons.

◄52

53. The unromantic side of U-boat service. Riding tiny steel splinters into the fiercest of waters, U-boatmen searched out their targets in all weathers. Almost always wet, and often freezing cold, lookouts stared between the swells for the elusive enemy. (Jochen Ahme via Ernst Schmidt)
54. *U-101* was one of five boats to particpate in one of the first experimental 'wolf-packs', the so-called 'First Wave'. *Gruppe Rösing* was formed in May 1940 and included *U-48* (after whose commander it was named), *U-29*, *U-43* and *U-46* as well as *U-101*. The group operated north-west of Cape Finisterre against convoy US-3 without success.
55. *U-29* sinking the Greek steamer *Adamastos*, 1 July 1940. After *Gruppe Rösing* broke up in mid-June 1940, *U-29* secretly entered El Ferrol to refuel from the German supply ship *Max Albrecht* and continued her patrol for another month before returning to Germany. During this patrol, Schuhart sank four ships totalling 26,000 tons. (SFL)

◄53 54▲ 55▼

▲56 ▼57

58▲

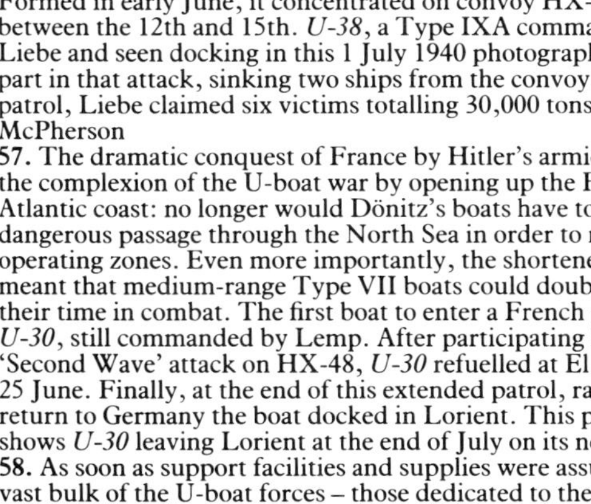

56. The second experimental 'wolf-pack' had better success. Formed in early June, it concentrated on convoy HX-48 between the 12th and 15th. *U-38*, a Type IXA commanded by Liebe and seen docking in this 1 July 1940 photograph, took part in that attack, sinking two ships from the convoy. For this patrol, Liebe claimed six victims totalling 30,000 tons. (Via Ken McPherson

57. The dramatic conquest of France by Hitler's armies changed the complexion of the U-boat war by opening up the French Atlantic coast: no longer would Dönitz's boats have to make the dangerous passage through the North Sea in order to reach their operating zones. Even more importantly, the shortened trip meant that medium-range Type VII boats could double or treble their time in combat. The first boat to enter a French port was *U-30*, still commanded by Lemp. After participating in the 'Second Wave' attack on HX-48, *U-30* refuelled at El Ferrol on 25 June. Finally, at the end of this extended patrol, rather than return to Germany the boat docked in Lorient. This photograph shows *U-30* leaving Lorient at the end of July on its next patrol.

58. As soon as support facilities and supplies were assured, the vast bulk of the U-boat forces – those dedicated to the Battle of the Atlantic – migrated to the French Atlantic ports: first Lorient, then Brest, St-Nazaire and La Pallice became home to Dönitz's flotillas. Here two boats of *7.Uflot* enter their new home-port of St-Nazaire

59. *U-37* enters Lorient, August 1940 (see also cover illustration). Dönitz took pains to see that U-boat crews were well received at their new foreign homes, both at the dockside and in town, where homes, bars and brothels were set up for the officers and crews.

◄59

▲60

60. Öhrn (foreground) relaxing at Kernaval, Dönitz's new headquarters in the Breton countryside. Here U-boat commanders could relax in comfort between patrols and get the latest information and instructions from Dönitz (seen in the background with the newspaper) and his staff. (John Albrecht)

61. The acquisition of the French ports opened new patrol areas for the longer-ranged U-boat types, and the first to be ordered into new waters was *UA*, which in June 1940 sortied into the South Atlantic. Seen here taking on supplies from *Pinguin* on 18 July, she continued operating in these tropical waters until early August. (SFL)

▼61

62. As might be expected, *UA's* return from this marathon patrol was jubilant, complete with brass band. The patrol was as successful as it was long, accounting for seven enemy ships. Her captain, Cohausz, was then replaced by Eckermann, but the former returned to command her for one final patrol in February 1942. (SFL)

63. Another '*Einbaum*' returns to port as *U-58*, a Type IIC, is greeted, 2 August 1940. Her commander at this time was Schonder. Like most of the '*Einbäume*', *U-58* was finally retired to training duties in December 1940.

62▲ 63▼

▲64 ▼65

64. Flying ten victory pennants, *U-48* draws into Lorient, 25 August 1940. This was Rösing's last patrol as commander of *U-48*. He was promoted to the command of all Atlantic boats (*FdU-West*), based at Angers.

65. The second sortie into the South Atlantic was every bit as successful as *UA*'s first experimental patrol. *U-65*, a Type IXB under von Stockhausen operated off Freetown, Sierra Leone, from 15 October 1940 to 10 January 1941, replenishing twice from *Nordmark*. For her efforts, she claimed nine victims, though was actually credited with eight ships totalling 47,000 tons.

66. 42,000 tons of Kretschmer's incredible total of tonnage sunk came during *U-99*'s fifth patrol, seen here ending on 10 November 1940 at St-Nazaire; Kretschmer, in a seaman's cap, is saluting from the tower. The pair of White Ensigns flying from the periscope commemorate a pair of auxiliary cruisers sunk by *U-99* in a running battle that lasted for seven hours.

66 ►

▲67

67. An unidentified early Type VIIC enters harbour. The experimental use of vanes to deflect spray around the edge of the tower is unusual. No satisfactory solution was ever found to the problem of deflecting spray and wind: U-boats were simply too low and too wet to avoid the problem, but the standard pattern of mid-tower and tower-edge deflectors was the best of a series of poor solutions. This particular design, however was not repeated.

68. The elation felt in Germany over the successes of the *Kriegsmarine*'s U-boats during the summer and autumn of 1940 was tempered, at least on the part of Dönitz, by the realization that so much more could have been achieved if only an adequate number of boats had been available. It was not until late in 1940 that the rushed construction programme belatedly initiated after war broke out began to have effect as new boats, particularly Type VIICs, were launched at a gradually increasing pace. This newly launched boat is seen at the Kriegsmarine Werft, Wilhelmshaven; it is one of the series *U-751* to *U-761*, these being the only Type VIIs built at that yard during this period. Note the builder's marks still visible at the bow and also the training flotilla insignia (a double diamond) on the tower.

▼68

69▲

69. Only after builder's trials, acceptance trials, necessary repairs and final inspection was a new U-boat turned over to the *Kriegsmarine* and commissioned. This photograph shows the climactic moment in the commissioning ceremony of *U-109*, the raising of the national ensign, on 5 December 1940. (Wolfgang Hirschfeld)

70. The veteran nucleus of the crew of a new boat assembled at the ship yard during the last months of construction, helping fit out the boat as it was being finished. This core was supplemented before the commissioning by newly trained recruits forwarded from training units, particularly the *U-bootslehrdivisionen* (ULD), to which most of those early '*Einbäume*' which had survived their stint in combat were retired in late 1940. Here *U-3* is seen in the markings of *ULD 'Pillau*'. The yellow band around the tower was common to all ULD boats. (John Albrecht)

70▼

▲71

71. The last of the '*Einbaum*' types, the Type IID, was the most capable, but it still suffered from an inadequate torpedo armament. These boats became operational late in 1940 and were generally kept in combat service only into 1941. In this view, the crew of a Type IID (probably *U-139*) gets instructions from its commander. The newness and uniformity of the crew's dress suggests that the photograph dates from the boat's working-up period.

72. *U-140*, another Type IID, at Lorient in February 1941. This submarine operated in the Atlantic from November 1940 to June 1941, at which time she was transferred, along with most of the other Type IIDs, to the Baltic for operations against Soviet shipping.

73. After a slack period caused by bad weather in the Atlantic, operations and successes mounted again in spring 1941. *U-96*, commanded by Lehmann-Willenbrock, is seen here at St-Nazaire on her return from patrol in March 1941. Operating west of Iceland with nine other U-boats against convoys HX-106 and HX-107, *U-96* sank three ships from the convoys and a total of nine ships on this patrol. Lehmann-Willenbrock was a successful commander (fifth on the tonnage list) and a popular one. He was promoted to the command of *9.Uflot* in April 1942. The well-known novel *Das Boot* by Lothar-Günther Buchheim is largely based on a patrol of *U-96* in November 1941 during which she re-supplied from the steamer *Bessel* in Vigo harbour and later attempted, unsuccessfully, to break through the Straits of Gibraltar. (Via Ken McPherson)

▼72

▼73

74▲

74. 'Wolf-pack' tactics were tried out in the South Atlantic in March and April 1941. *U-105* (seen here entering Lorient flying twelve victory pennants), *U-103* and *U-107* operated in consort off Freetown during this period, harassing one convoy, SL-68, for three nights (between 17 and 19 March), sinking seven ships and causing its dispersal. While on this patrol, *U-105* was replenished several times from *Kormoran*, *Nordmark* and *Corrientes*.

75. *U-94*, a Type VIIC commanded by Kuppisch, docks at St-Nazaire after an eventful patrol, May 1941. During the course of this sortie, *U-94* attacked the convoys SC-26 and OB-318, was damaged by depth charges from the escorting destroyers and later attempted to support the battleship *Bismarck*'s disastrous death ride. In all, Kuppisch was credited with seven ships totalling almost 43,000 tons.

75▼

76. Docking after a patrol, Kuppisch and the tower watch of *U-94* present an interesting spectacle. The variety and informality of uniform were characteristic of the U-boat service, and the bowler hats and ski-cap seen here may have been eccentric but certainly were not extreme. The painting of a bedraggled-looking seabird hanging within the DF loop was, however, an unusual decoration.
77. *U-93*, a Type VIIC commanded by Korth, enters St-Nazaire, 3 May 1941. In company with *U-94*, Korth had attacked the convoy OB-318 and two others, but the absence of victory pennants tells its story.
78. *U-123* docking at Lorient on 11 May 1941. The decoration and camouflage shown here were not unusual except for the boat's insignia, which represents an infantryman's medal. This was unique both in that it was a representation of an Army medal and in that it explictly includes a swastika – in general, such a specifically Nazi decoration rarely appeared on U-boats. After this patrol, *U-123*'s commander, Möhle, turned the boat over to Hardegen, who had much greater success with her.
79. During her working-up period in the Baltic, *U-556* had occasion to cross paths with the battleship *Bismarck* engaged in the same activity. In rather impertinent fashion, Wohlfarth, *U-556*'s commander, announced that his boat was 'adopting' the giant dreadnought as her 'godson'. On her first patrol, *U-556* found herself in a position to help the wounded giant: the British battle group attacking *Bismarck* sailed within her sights on 27 May 1941, but *U-556* had no torpedoes. This view shows her return to Lorient three days later, her crew in sombre mood despite the eight victory pennants flying from her periscope and the claim of 49,500 tons painted on her tower.
◀76

77▲

78▲ 79▼

▲80

80. *U-556* alongside her tender at Lorient, 30 May 1941. Note the broad stripe-pattern camouflage. On her next patrol, the boat was sunk by depth charges off Iceland, losing four of her crew.

81. The great successes achieved in the South Atlantic, where the escorts were fewer and the convoy system was not nearly as strictly enforced, led to a sharp increase in the number of boats assigned to the region during the late spring of 1941. Along with decreased defences, naturally, came a greater scarcity of targets, and weeks would pass without a single target being sighted: here the tower watch on *U-109* scans an empty sea in the hope of locating a victim. Unaccustomed to the harsh tropical sun, many of the watch crew acquired pith helmets for protection. (Wolfgang Hirschfield)

▼81

82▲

82. Because of the relative scarcity of targets, it was only by extending the length of patrols that good success rates could be acheived – and the only way to extend patrols was through replenishment on the high seas. One such rendezvous is seen here: *U-107*, a Type IXB commanded by Hessler (one of two U-boat commanders who were also sons-in-law of Dönitz), takes on supplies from *Nordmark* (disguised as the American freighter *Prairie*), 19 June 1941. Such rendezvous were obviously dangerous for all the participants.

83. The re-supply system was most important for the shorter-ranged Type VIIs, such as *U-29*, seen here from *U-107* at Punkt Rot, one of the established rendezvous points, 19 June 1941. Without such re-supply, the Type VIIs would have been able to spend only a few days on station off Freetown before being forced to return.

83▼

▲84

▲85 ▼86

84. Docking at St-Nazaire on 10 June 1941, *U-93* ends a sadly abbreviated patrol. As a result of the greatly increased U-boat activity off Freetown, the British made the destruction of the German South Atlantic re-supply network a top priority. In the first fortnight of June, five of the re-supply ships were captured or sunk by British cruisers. *U-93* had been in the act of refuelling from *Belchen* on 3 June when the cruisers appeared. She was able to submerge in time but *Belchen* was sunk. Surfacing later, the submarine picked up 50 of *Belchen*'s crew (seen on deck aft of the tower) and returned them safely to France.

85. The most successful U-boat of the war, *U-48*, completed its final combat patrol in June 1941, once again under the command of 'Vaddi' Schultze. The claimed tonnage had now reached a staggering 401,623. Postwar analysis reduced this by 91,000 tons, but still left an impressive total. After this patrol, *U-48* was retired to school-ship duties in the Baltic.

86. U-boat insignia were derived from a multitude of different sources, from crests and coats of arms of cities or families, from legends or folk tales, from good (or bad) luck symbols like a horseshoe or a black cat, from naval academy class insignia or from some personal token that held meaning for the captain or crew. In general, they tried to evoke some noble, aggressive or even humorous quality that helped to give to the crew and show to the outside world some notion of the unique characteristics of the particular boat. How, then, is *U-69*'s insignia to be explained? It was adopted from the corporate logo of a French cheese manufacturer. Maybe food was really the most important thing to a U-boatman!

87–89. *U-48*'s insignia, the black cat, showed up in a multitude of different locations. It was displayed on a plaque resting on the forward radio antenna. It was made into a stuffed toy displayed along with a rather well executed carving of a sea nymph (we know what else U-boatmen thought about besides food on those long patrols) on *U-48*'s tower. It even became the emblem of a band entertaining at one of the sailor's rest homes.

87▲

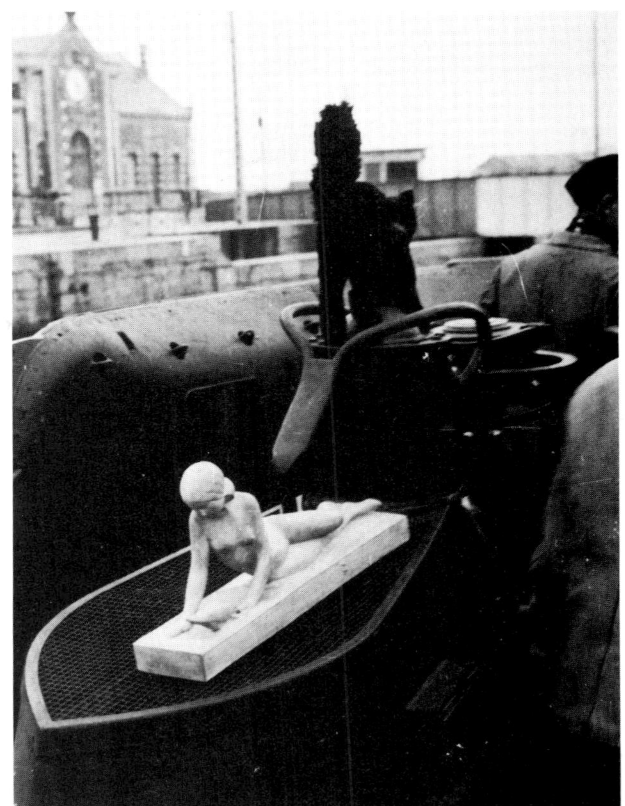

88▲ 89▼

▲90 ▼91

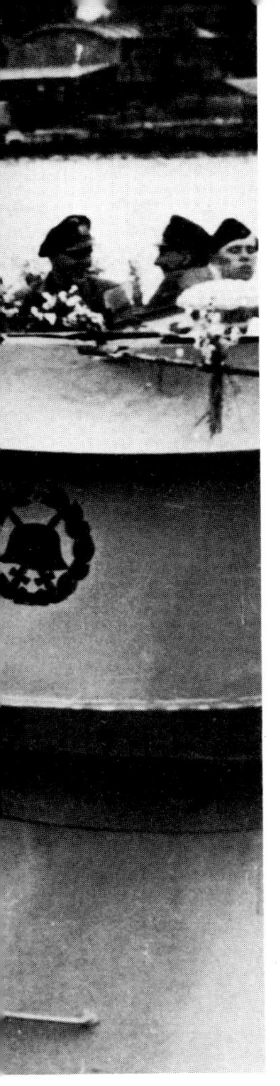

90. A pair of famous boats returns to Lorient, 8 June 1941: *U-123* is in the foreground, *U-201* in the background. Under Hardegen, *U-123* became an aggressive and successful boat, the sixth most successful in terms of tonnage sunk. Hardegen retained the original ship's insignia chosen by Möhle, although it was not unusual for a new captain to substitute his own insignia for an old one in an attempt to place a personal 'stamp' on the boat.
91. A close-up view of *U-123*'s tower with *U-201* in the background. Flowers were a traditional decoration on a returning boat's tower, but much more important to the crew was the fresh food waiting upon their return. Note the elaborately decorated cake and the lobsters on *U-123*'s tower, while *U-201* displays an elaborate camouflage pattern of dark stripes. Hardegen, in the white cap to the left, wears a British battle-dress blouse, a popular item of clothing among U-boatmen.
92. *U-201*'s commander was Dönitz's other son-in-law, 'Adi' Schnee. After giving up command of *U-201* in September 1942, he joined his father-in-law's staff under Eberhardt Godt, Dönitz's chief of operations throughout the war.
93. *UA* docking at Lorient, 30 July 1941, after another long patrol off Freetown, her commander at this time being Eckermann. Her tower structure was unique among German-built U-boats because of the Turkish reqirement that the deck gun be carried high in the tower; the breech of the gun is just visible to the left in this view. That much weight carried high in the tower led to some unpleasant roll characteristics, causing the boat to wallow in any but the calmest sea – hence the whale insignia.

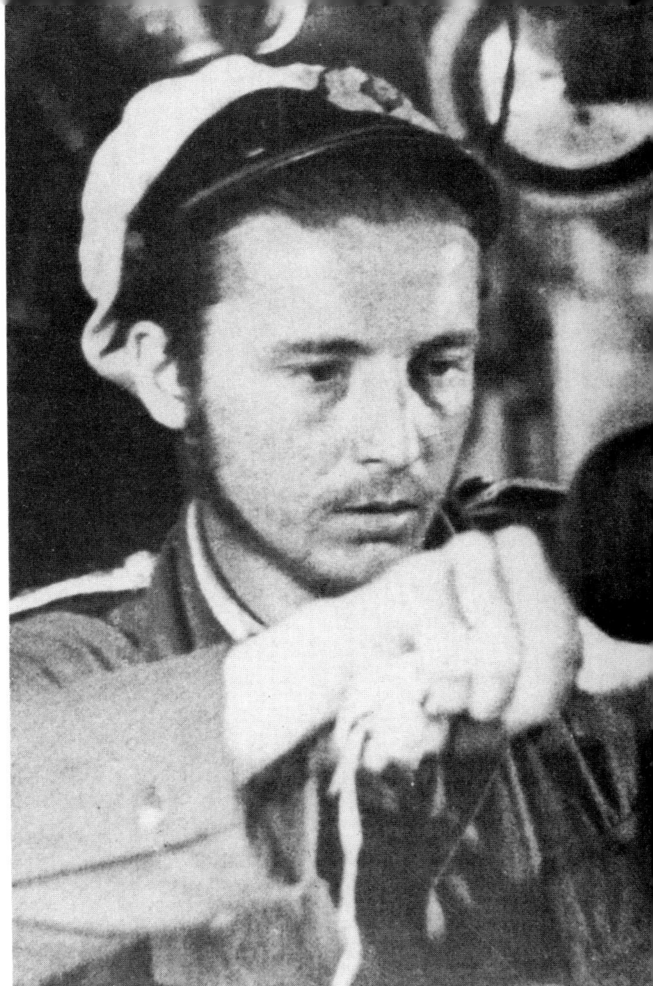

92▲ 93▼

▲94

94. An unidentified Type IX, possibly *U-123*, draws alongside *UA* at Lorient, 2 August 1941. These were the relatively carefree days before the regular British air bombardment of French ports forced all activities under the shelter of hardened concrete U-boat pens.
95. More arrivals at Lorient, 25 August 1941. *U-126*, commanded by Bauer, has just returned from a patrol off Gibraltar, four victory pennants attesting to success in those waters, while another Type IX, possibly *U-131*, approaches in the background. The bulge on the side of *U-126*'s tower was a housing for an extendible long-range radio antenna that was being fitted to all U-boats.
96. *U-109* under her second commander, Bleichrodt (in the white scarf), enters Lorient. In August 1941, this boat completed an extended patrol off Gibraltar, during which she was re-supplied from the tanker *Thalia* in Cadiz harbour on 22 July. (Wolfgang Hirschfeld)
97. *U-570* was an unlucky boat. She had an unpopular commander, and she suffered more than her fair share of mechanical teething problems during her work-up. This training period was cut short, from the regular five or six months to only two, in an experimental attempt to get more new boats into combat before the onset of winter slowed operations. The results were disastrous. Damaged by a Hudson bomber off Iceland, *U-570* surrendered to the aircraft on 29 August 1941. Seen in this photograph at Reykjavik shortly thereafter, *U-570* was commissioned into the Royal Navy as *HMS Graph* on 19 September. (Via Ken McPherson)

▼95

96 ▲ 97 ▼

▲98 ▼99

98. *U-130*, a new Type IXC, at Lorient at the conclusion of her first patrol, late summer 1941. Her commander at the time of her commissioning was Kals. The absence of victory pennants indicates that this first patrol, which started from Kiel, could be chalked up as a learning experience. (Ed Rumpf)
99. On her next try, *U-130* had more success, as evidenced by the four victory pennants. The heavy coats worn by the tower crew indicate that the winter is now coming on, accompanied by a general worsening of the weather at sea and a corresponding reduction in victories. *U-130*, along with a number of other boats, had two different insignia. That carried on the port side, just visible here, is probably the crest of a city that sponsored the boat – a fairly common type of decoration; the knight's head insignia was probably Kal's own.
100. Entering St-Nazaire on 19 November 1941, *U-95* flies no victory pennants. This patrol was another victim of the worsening weather conditions and stiffening defences encountered in the Atlantic in late autumn 1941. On her next patrol *U-95* was ordered to break through into the Mediterranean. There she was torpedoed by the Dutch submarine *O.21* just east of Gibraltar on 28 November.
101. *U-128*, a new Type IXC, at Lorient on Christmas Eve 1941. As the threat from Allied attack, particularly from the air, increased towards the end of the year, it became more common to see camouflaged U-boats (note the camouflage striping even on the periscope heads). The muzzle of a 7.92mm machine gun is visible behind the captain: the fitting of a rifle-calibre machine gun to the tower was a first, halting step towards increasing the 'flak' armament of U-boats.

100▲

101▼

▲102 ▼103

102. *U-124* flying at least eight victory pennants and also exhibiting a life-belt upon which is painted its victory claims, one destroyer and 39,000 tons sunk on this patrol. (The tonnage of *naval* vessels sunk was omitted from the total tonnage claimed – an indication of the absolute emphasis by Dönitz on the sinking of merchant shipping.) *U-124* under Schulz and later Mohr continued these triumphs, going on to become the fourth most successful boat of the war.
103. Despite the polar bear insignia, *U-108* spent most of the second half of 1941 patrolling the South Atlantic off Freetown and Gibraltar. It was from this latter region that she was returning in this view taken on Christmas Day at Lorient.

104▲ 105▼

104. The reception for *U-751* at St-Nazaire included a Christmas tree. She deserved the elaborate welcome because on this patrol she claimed the sinking of the *Audacity* on 21 December, the first of the Royal Navy's escort carriers. *Audacity* had been escorting the convoy HG-76 when *U-751*, part of *Gruppe Seeräuber*, hit her with a single torpedo. That stopped her, but it took two more torpedoes 70 minutes later finally to send her to the bottom.

105. Late in the year, four boats – *UA*, *U-68*, *U-124* and *U-129* – were involved in an accident similar to that experienced by *U-93* back in June. *UA*, along with *U-68*, was refuelling from *Python* in the South Atlantic when they were surprised by British cruisers on 1 December. The story was the same. Again the supply ship was sunk but the U-boats were able to submerge in time. They later surfaced and picked up survivors from *Python* (including also survivors of *Atlantis* which had itself been sunk on 22 November). This view shows *U-68* (foreground) and *UA* entering Lorient on Christmas Day 1941, jammed with survivors of the two supply ships. *U-68*'s five victory pennants include two victims sunk in Walvis Bay.

106, 107. After *U-37* was retired to training duties in March 1941, her last commander, 'Nico' Claussen, was sent to work up the newly completed *U-129*. He took *U-37*'s famous 'Westward Ho!' emblem with him. Seen here docking on Christmas Day 1941, *U-129* also participated in the rescue of some 414 survivors from *Atlantis* and *Python*. She was very experienced in this type of operation, having also been involved in the rescue of all 119 survivors of the tanker *Kota Pinang* in October. With the loss of these ships, the German South Atlantic re-supply network ceased to exist.

▲**106** ▼**107**

108, 109. The last of the rescue ships to reach port was *U-124*, which docked on 29 December 1941. She flies two victory pennants, one representing the American steamer *Sagadahoc* – now that the Japanese had precipitously brought the United States into the war, American targets were fair game. The other was for the British cruiser *Dunedin*, one of the cruisers that had been decimating the South Atlantic supply network – a small measure of revenge for the damage done to the *Kriegsmarine*'s U-boat offensive in the South Atlantic. Until the appearance of the Type XB and Type XIVA supply U-boats in mid-1942, the South Atlantic would be open to only the longest-ranged submarines.

108▲ 109▼

▲110 ▼111

110. Despite the vigorous objections of Dönitz, Hitler ordered U-boats into the Mediterranean in an attempt to support the German land forces in North Africa. *U-79*, seen here at Brest on 17 August 1941, was one of six boats formed into *Gruppe Göben* that was instructed to break through the Straits of Gibraltar. All six boats (*U-75*, *U-97*, *U-331*, *U-371* and *U-559*, as well as *U-79*) safely made the passage through the Straits between 24 September and 5 October and gathered at Salamis, their first operational base in the Mediterranean.

111. *U-97* was another member of *Gruppe Göben*; she is seen here at St-Nazaire just prior to breaking into the Mediterranean. As with all other boats that were assigned to the Mediterranean, *U-97* remained there until her loss. This was the reason for Dönitz's futile objections to assigning boats to the Mediterranean: he knew that any boats so assigned would be permanently removed from the primary theatre of operations, the Atlantic.

112. Guggenberger's *U-81* joined the boats in the Mediterranean, slipping through the Straits of Gibraltar on 12 November 1941. Within 24 hours she had stumbled upon a British task force which included the fleet carrier *Ark Royal*. Before being forced to dive by the escort, she managed to get four torpedoes away, one of which hit the carrier. At first the damage appeared to be non-fatal and the carrier was taken under tow, but during the night uncontrollable fires ravaged the ship and she sank the next morning only 25 miles from Gibraltar. This photograph shows *U-81* entering Salamis after her twelfth patrol.

113. The most dramatic victory came to *Freiherr* von Tiesenhausen's *U-331* when she torpedoed the old battleship HMS *Barham* on 25 November 1941. Hit by three torpedoes, *Barham* began to capsize almost immediately, and within five minutes, already lying on her beam's end, was torn apart by a magazine explosion. In commemoration of victory, an appropriate silhouette was painted on the inner door of No. 1 torpedo tube in *U-331*'s forward torpedo room.

112▲ 113▼

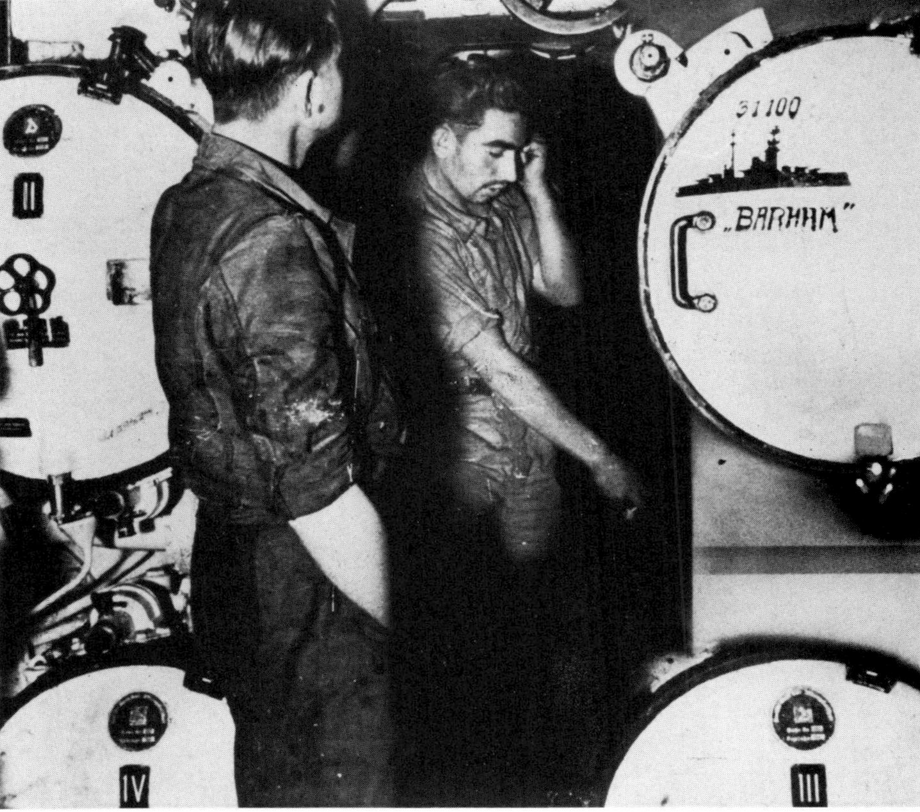

114. *U-77* at Lorient on 10 December 1941, just before breaking into the Mediterranean. On her way to Gibraltar *U-77* took part in *Gruppe Seeräuber*'s attack on the convoy HG-76, claiming one steamer of almost 5,000 tons on 15 December 1941. Once in the Mediterranean, she sank the destroyer HMS *Kimberley* on 12 January 1942, the first of three destroyers claimed by the submarine in 1942.

115. U-boats were transferred to another theatre in 1941, but this was one to which Dönitz had no objections. In support of the invasion of Russia, Hitler wanted a U-boat presence in the Black Sea. Accordingly six Type IIB '*Einbäume*', for which Dönitz had little other use, were transported by canal and road to the Donau (Danube) and then by barge to Galati, Romania. One of the six is seen here in autumn 1941 on the autobahn near Dresden. (SLF)

▲114 ▼115

116. The recommissioning of the Type IIBs in the Black Sea took some time. The first to be brought back into service was *U-24*, seen here in the Black Sea some time after her recommissioning on 14 October 1942. She sports a graded camouflage scheme worn by all six Black Sea boats. Targets were never plentiful in those restricted waters, but the anti-submarine forces were limited and the boats had considerable success. *U-24* completed ten patrols before she was scuttled to avoid capture at Constantia, 25 August 1944.

117. The most famous of the Black Sea boats was *U-9*, the first command of Lüth, who went on to become the second most successful U-boat commander. She was recommissioned at Galati, still sporting the Iron Cross insignia on her tower, and she remained active in the Black Sea until sunk by air attack in Constantia on 20 August 1944.

118. *U-19* was recommissioned at Galati on 28 December 1942. She conducted nine patrols against Soviet shipping and naval forces until she was scuttled on 10 September 1944, her commander and three of her crew being interned in Turkey for the remainder of the war. (SLF)

116▲

117▲ 118▼

▲119

▲120 ▼121

119. *U-18* in the Black Sea. She was recommissioned there on 6 May 1943, subsequently conducting seven patrols. She, too, was scuttled at Constantia to avoid capture on 25 August 1944.

120. The crew of *U-20* stands for inspection by her commander, Schöler, soon after the boat's recommissioning on 27 May 1943. Besides her 'personal' insignia, she carries the Olympic Rings, indicating that one of her commanders was a member of a naval academy class that graduated at the time of the Berlin Olympics. The personal insignia shows a folk figure known as 'Hans im Gluck'. *U-20* also conducted seven patrols before being scuttled off the Turkish coast on 10 September 1944.

121. *U-23* at Constantia. She was the last of the six Black Sea boats to be reactivated, joining the others on 3 June 1943. She also was scuttled on 10 September 1944 off the Turkish coast as the last German-held ports fell to advancing Soviets troops.